The poems in *Teeth & Teeth* risk simplicity—of the line, of language, and ultimately of desire. Language here is not fantastical or flexed, but quiet and intentional, precise—language is allowed to feel, to labor, to pulse. Because of this, the poems' momentous hunger, anger, desire—the poems' "teeth" if you will—are urgently and deceivingly near. As in "Desire Diary," the desire is imperfect and inexplicable, a machine, even: "Inside the mechanism, everyone / was handsome. Everyone / Came at it with a strange green / sound leaking from their / Lips." The momentum of desire in *Teeth & Teeth*—for a mother, a memory, a lover, a knowing, a world—is palpable and fast.
—Natalie Diaz, judge of the Charlotte Mew Prize

"Grief creates its own fire," writes Reagler in "Re-Routed," part of a collection devastating and warm, dazzling, clarifying, unpredictable, and which feels inevitable. What sustenance there is in finding language that speaks of inadequacy as a beginning and of faith as faith's absence. Through the poems we inhabit the void, our efforts to fill it, and affirm desire as unexpected fulfillment in itself.
—Martha Serpas

Robin Reagler's *Teeth & Teeth* is a wild-mouthed dispatch from the cities of mourning we all inhabit, a desperate love letter to the waiting selves which grow out of exile from normalcy. In the face of the wearing down of the body, despite loss, these poems demand gratitude for the fierce habits of the living.
—Ching-In Chen

Teeth & Teeth

Teeth & Tenth

Teeth & Teeth

Robin Reagler

HEADMISTRESS PRESS

Copyright © 2018 by Robin Reagler
All rights reserved.

ISBN-13: 978-0999593004
ISBN-10: 0999593005

This book may not be reproduced, in whole or in part, including illustrations, in any form (beyond that permitted by Sections 107 and 108 of the U.S. Copyright Law and except by reviewers for the public press), without written permission from the publishers.

Cover & book design by Mary Meriam
Cover art by Hilma af Klint, Altarpiece No. 3, 1915

PUBLISHER
Headmistress Press
60 Shipview Lane
Sequim, WA 98382
Telephone: 917-428-8312
Email: headmistresspress@gmail.com
Website: headmistresspress.blogspot.com

In memory of my father
In honor of my mother
And for Marcia, Pearl, and Carrie, with all my love

Struck by the abstract nature of absence; yet it's so painful, lacerating. Which allows me to understand abstraction somewhat better: it is absence and pain, the pain of absence—perhaps therefore love?

—Roland Barthes, *Mourning Diary*
tr. Richard Howard

CONTENTS

FEAR. DESIRE. FIRE.	1
NOBODY'S CHILDREN	2
THE CUTTING HOUR	3
THE WAY	4
RE-ROUTED	5
WE HOLY THIEVES	7
ALTERNATE NAMES FOR G-D	8
GRIEF. SEX. MOURNING.	9
I AM KNEELING	11
DESIRE DIARY	13
POEM THAT I CAN'T FINISH	15
TEETH & TEETH	17
DNR - DO NOT RESUSCITATE	18
HIS TOMBSTONE	20
SANCTUARY, OR I'M BLEEDING	22
ALTERNATE NAMES FOR US	23
ABOUT THE AUTHOR	25

FEAR. DESIRE. FIRE.

Deep inside me, the hawks
Are circling. Again. Their
Single-mindedness blitzes in
And prepares for some kind
Of fight. With effort I manage
To control my face, but I
Carefully avoid the cameras.
I walk as though I am
Not completely visible. When
I arrive before you, it is as
An acolyte, waiting to be
Taught. I dream of escaping
The terror that I might
Simply become. There are many
Ways to tell any story.
My body is the lesbian body.
And when in darkness you
Come to me, I struggle
To believe you're real.
Then I, the self who is
Nobody, begin to burn,
And I am lit up and wed
To the fields on fire.
That is called flying,
And there is nothing
Like it. Nothing before
It. Nothing after it.

NOBODY'S CHILDREN

It's impossible to predict

Cloud-shaped names   Pillow names

how the stranded feel regret

and they don't realize

they are hunted

Destiny names   Linear names

Their desire is expressed

in precise parallel lines

cut into their forearms

Camouflage names   Commando names

Transcending from pain

to lightness to

a steadiness of breath

Remaining names   Becoming names

as their bodies unreel a list of what

we have lost that can never be replaced

THE CUTTING HOUR

More nowhere than a fever

Stronger than a sparrow

The song of the railroad train

Lulls us to sleep if you listen

Yes, the first evening knows

The heart knows early on

The blood cells scream out knowledge

And falling   not falling   falling again

I am we are you will be

Like a tourniquet, mostly alive

At the border of two stories

THE WAY

I know, while peeling the clementines

for them, that they are ripe. The way fingernails

grow secretly or not at all. The way

she says the word *terraces,* and it sounds

like *terrorists.* The way smoke travels

lazily from one mouth to another.

The way stories bleed as they sing.

The way the cat sleeps in my spot

on the bed, with his head half-hidden

beneath his shadowy paw. The way I pray

sleep will drape itself over me like a living

mountain of curtain. The way I die

with my father every night, over and over,

holding his dry and weightless hand.

RE-ROUTED

I am not you. Just placed here by you. My body that came from your bodies.

The prayer *Kaddish* enters me, a bullet between my teeth. Briefly, all my cells

can curse. Then you both disappear, traveling a road that was never there. As in

calculus, the road becomes a non-place in steady motion. It is represented by

the letter Y.

Upward,

outward,

skyward.

And we,

opening

our eyes,

are surprised by the incandescence that outlines every mountain, every cliff and tor.

Grief creates its own fire. Its own revelation. My parents, two silver dots on a temporary

paper map. And traveler, although we have only just met, your fate is mine. Once fate

flares up into horizon, you will understand why I am taking another crash course in dust signaling

pathways

for the dead,

as the skinny

child

is running

through

the fields, brandishing a willow branch and condemning the beauty of a perfect day.

WE HOLY THIEVES

At night I write to you
Because the moon's fullness
Is a bad accident, and I
Need to travel halfway
Across Texas, driving
In reverse. Our love
Is a screech owl; we
Agree on that
Much. I'm miles past
Livingston, past
Nacogdoches. The darkness
Gasps with the blush
Of sunrise. Nobody
Recognizes what is
So obviously blooming.
The beautiful part   is you.

ALTERNATE NAMES FOR G-D

Rock	Rocked	Clock house
Duck decoy	Brakes	Outer space
Lob	Fake lake	Grief
Pop of comic book color		Drop cloth
Boomerang	Blame	Love-proof
Asleep in an instant		
Mobility	From earth	From fire
Motility	Inertia	Eclipse
Moot Court	Language	Anger
Twang	Desire	Desired
Teeth	Awake in the desert	
Owl	Uneven screech	
Moon	Sharpened edge	

GRIEF. SEX. MOURNING.

There was no twang in the system   so I hurled it

into the fire   My mother kept scratching

an itch that infuriated   every cell of her

dying   which for her must have been

a kind of perhaps   a kind of dry fire a burning

with death   the only possible

healing

     No doubt I am guilty

as hell   for this human interpretation

Or else you must see me   so clearly that

       like the flow of electrons

that completes the circuit   this

is an ending, this   is all there is

I will   ask you a question

you already   memorized your answer

Desire cripples me

you know   what I need

I am humble humiliated fueled

by my own despair as I beg you

I beg you

lust instructs me and there's a turntable, with that scat song

    repeating the pain repeating the pain a rhythmic

witness to this most recent test of our love

    fastening, unfastening the already pounding of our bodies

I AM KNEELING

People who do not tell their stories

keep quiet to tighten up time.

I haven't suffered as much as you.

My thoughts are wrong and hardly mine.

In dreams you are pregnant, and as I hold

my palm to the globe of your belly,

fear stiches my mouth shut.

When it comes to us, I am confused.

The ocean is human is a flying among stars.

My mother has left behind her living

body, and it somehow knows my name.

I haven't suffered as much as you.

On TV there's always a new disaster

with people shouting lies and

shooting bullets at one another.

I'm not sure why I love you.

In the park my aloneness does

not stand out so much.

Dogs sniff each other, then play.

How is it they know what they know?

I walk for hours until I can't any more,

kicking up dust from earth to heaven.

All the park benches, empty, and over-

head the hawks circle us without any

effort, as though it's the easiest way.

DESIRE DIARY

Inside the mechanism, everyone

        was handsome. Everyone

Came at it with a strange green

        sound leaking from their

Lips. At 4 a.m. she sensed a classic

        case of slash and burn.

It was decided she would be slash,

        I, burn. In this way

Generosity became organized into

        compartments, and we

Could take turns reading

        the ransomed air.

Which is to say. Now we lie on our backs

        in the hotel bed catching

Our breath thinking that nothing

        is as pure as this nothingness,

While the sash of sleep coils around

        our lips and wrists, binding

Us, the pure, the forgetful

        we were when this

Ritual began. It's how—

        around, and down—

We end up where we began.

POEM THAT I CAN'T FINISH

Today I didn't write you

because I was mind-muddled

with the sounds of the railroad

trains in the yard I refused

to sign my name I

felt my limbs as though

they weren't really mine

and in a moment of double vision

having forgotten to eat

I began to write

so here's a poem for

the emptiness of days

when the body remembers

exactly what it can or will contain,

like an addition problem

without an actual total

Am I lonely? I ask

my lungs *Aren't I ready?*

I ask my legs

because although I make myself

love-proof, I won't be touched

in that way again, I will never

touch you in that way. I

am a promise This is

a poem about the story

you never told me It's

the untold stories with gigantic

hawk wings that swoop back over me

darkening the breathable air

and turning to dirty steam, the speed

of that memory, illegal,

the tell as I walk alone along

the train tracks, ignoring the pennies

stretched to three times their size,

looking upward to greet

the bellowing thunderstorm that never

TEETH & TEETH

We were born in Memphis, embalmed and verified,

angry and problematic, a feeling of flatness, a glow

of radiation, in the shade, hatred. The two fighters, Tyson,

Lewis, salsa in the ring, fighting, the faces like secrets

behind their red boxing gloves. Could their glaring be the look

of love? The end-all of love? Jabbing at the injustice of each damn

day, the two men roar toward one another. How much $$$ would you

pay for a left hook to the jaw, a bite in the leg, the taste of blood,

as Tyson, free of his mouth guard, is seized by a moment

of perfect vampire. So that we are a Basquiat painting of scraped

marrow and uncontained fire. We are the symbiosis of politics and outrage.

Uppercut. Knockout. 21st century America thrust into motion.

DNR - DO NOT RESUSCITATE

Some days I am an atheist

taking a crash course in dust.

The cold seeps into the house

through the windows and hard-

wood floors. Sentences. In cold

hard sentences I think about

my mother, even when

I'm not thinking about her

at all. She and her body

that isn't hers any more.

I feel fear in my teeth,

then my childhood blooms.

I'm the boy prince of every

weed and bug in the gullies.

My brother and I know

each dip and ditch of this.

Now my brother is laughing,

and I'm racing uphill with a swarm

of hornets forming a crown

in my hair. My very loneliness

flips over and spills out

across the kitchen table.

I am eleven. Mom makes

a paste of water and baking

soda and rubs it into my

head. It dries white in my

black curls. She leaves me

to dry in sunshine. You weren't

there, although I'd begun

to imagine you. And now? I can't

stop thinking about your hands.

HIS TOMBSTONE

Skies are flying. I, wild
As the flowers, wild
As birds escaping

Sudden knowledge.
Somehow it's been a year
Since we planted my father

Into this hill, and somehow
I keep hurting myself without
Meaning it. Pain is G-d's season too.

Clouds rake the sky,
And I taste the thunder,
Almost metallic, like

Clams. If I feel fine,
Why do my ears keep
Bleeding. What is the

Noise coming from that raft
Of hot air. Lightning
Clears a path for us.

There. I am breathing
Again. But mesmerizing
Me, terribly far away,

My father. Am I still
Able to assemble
His voice, his face.

Memory's drumming
Carries a message to us, the
Mourners. We are

Clocks within hearts
As we glide through
The February graveyard.

SANCTUARY, OR I'M BLEEDING

Because I sleep face-down, I am

night's sister, I am death's husband,

I am the whore of the Lord. I wake up

sore and tired, remembering a girl

in France. I watch her sitting

upright on the wooden pew singing

a psalm that expresses all that I am

        grief   sex   mourning

           fear   desire fire

in a medieval church. Why has she

come for me? The wind, the naked

wind, has a voice that ticks. I am

alone, and the long line of time

ceases to breathe. Sunrise will never

arrive. Squinting, I wish for hell. It swims up

brightly and fills me with wonder.

ALTERNATE NAMES FOR US

On one such flammable night
when the stars no longer conspire
against me, I
arrive at her throat,
lips ready to press my love into skin, to
ignite a blaze in her nerve endings,

and somehow grief swings a 180
so that instead of her, again I'm thinking about my-
self, my mouth swimming inside
hers, my desire erasing
her need from the dashboard of
what-even-is. I

struggle to reclaim some gritty sense of
this woman I love. But it is losing
upon losing, another rendition
of Let's Get Lost. We twist
with violence and beauty
in the rounding-out space
of our one, our single body,
twinning.

ABOUT THE AUTHOR

Robin Reagler is a poet and educator living in Houston, Texas. She is also the author of *Dear Red Airplane* (Seven Kitchens Press, 2011), which will be re-issued in 2018. Her poems have appeared in *Ploughshares, Pleiades, Iowa Review, Colorado Review,* and other journals. She earned an MFA from the Iowa Writers' Workshop and a PhD from the University of Houston Creative Writing Program. She serves as the Executive Director of Writers in the Schools (WITS) and leads the national WITS Alliance.

HEADMISTRESS PRESS BOOKS

Lovely - Lesléa Newman
Teeth & Teeth - Robin Reagler
How Distant the City - Freesia McKee
Shopgirls - Marissa Higgins
Riddle - Diane Fortney
When She Woke She Was an Open Field - Hilary Brown
God With Us - Amy Lauren
A Crown of Violets - Renée Vivien tr. Samantha Pious
Fireworks in the Graveyard - Joy Ladin
Social Dance - Carolyn Boll
The Force of Gratitude - Janice Gould
Spine - Sarah Caulfield
Diatribe from the Library - Farrell Greenwald Brenner
Blind Girl Grunt - Constance Merritt
Acid and Tender - Jen Rouse
Beautiful Machinery - Wendy DeGroat
Odd Mercy - Gail Thomas
The Great Scissor Hunt - Jessica K. Hylton
A Bracelet of Honeybees - Lynn Strongin
Whirlwind @ Lesbos - Risa Denenberg
The Body's Alphabet - Ann Tweedy
First name Barbie last name Doll - Maureen Bocka
Heaven to Me - Abe Louise Young
Sticky - Carter Steinmann
Tiger Laughs When You Push - Ruth Lehrer
Night Ringing - Laura Foley
Paper Cranes - Dinah Dietrich
On Loving a Saudi Girl - Carina Yun
The Burn Poems - Lynn Strongin
I Carry My Mother - Lesléa Newman
Distant Music - Joan Annsfire
The Awful Suicidal Swans - Flower Conroy
Joy Street - Laura Foley
Chiaroscuro Kisses - G.L. Morrison
The Lillian Trilogy - Mary Meriam
Lady of the Moon - Amy Lowell, Lillian Faderman, Mary Meriam
Irresistible Sonnets - ed. Mary Meriam
Lavender Review - ed. Mary Meriam

www.ingramcontent.com/pod-product-compliance
Lightning Source LLC
Chambersburg PA
CBHW070045070426
42449CB00012BA/3166